D1196429

MOUNTAIN

MOUNTAIN

MOUNTAIN
The Journey of Justice Douglas

BY

DOUGLAS SCOTT

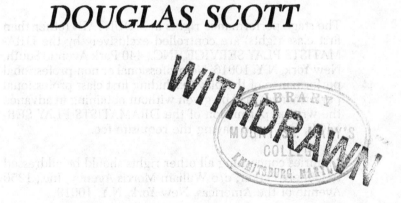

GARDEN CITY, NY

Photographs © Copyright 1990 by Martha Swope
Design by Maria Chiarino
Manufactured in the United States of America

Quality Printing and Binding by:
Berryville Graphics
P.O. Box 272
Berryville, VA 22611 U.S.A.

MOUNTAIN was initially produced as a staged reading at Lucille Lortel's White Barn Theatre in Westport, Connecticut and had its world premiere at the George Street Playhouse in New Brunswick, New Jersey, Gregory S. Hurst, Producing Artistic Director. MOUNTAIN opened off-Broadway at the Lucille Lortel Theatre in New York City on April 5, 1990, produced by K & D Productions/Margery Klain and Robert G. Donnalley, Jr., in association with Lucille Lortel. MOUNTAIN was directed by John Henry Davis, the set was designed by Philipp Jung, the costumes by David C. Woolard, the lighting by Dennis Parichy, the score and sound by John Gromada. James Fitzsimmons was production stage manager. The cast was as follows:

William O. Douglas . . . . Len Cariou
Man . . . . John C. Vennema
Woman . . . . Heather Summerhayes

CAST OF CHARACTERS

William O. Douglas
Man: FDR, Gordon Hirabayashi, Jasper Crisbody,
              Richard Nixon, Amir Ahmadi, Louis
              Brandeis and other memories
Woman: Julia Fisk Douglas, Mildred Riddle
              Douglas, Mercedes Davidson Douglas,
              Catherine Heffernan Douglas and other
              memories

> *"To live is to struggle with the demons*
> *that infest the heart and the head*
> *And to sit in Last Judgment*
> *on one's Self."*
>
> —HENRIK IBSEN

Although the play begins and ends at the time of his death, it spans most of the eighty-one years of William O. Douglas' life: as Justice on the Supreme Court; as chairman of the SEC and professor at Columbia and Yale; on his globe–trotting journeys to such lands as Iran and the Himalayas; and his childhood in the Cascade Mountains of Washington State.

Some passages in this play are freely adapted from sections of the following books: William O. Douglas' *Strange Lands and Friendly People*, 1951; and James F. Simon's *Independent Journey*, 1980 (used by permission of Harper & Row Publishers, Inc.); and William O. Douglas' *Beyond the High Himalayas*, 1952; *West of the Indus*, 1958; *My Wilderness*, 1961; *Go East, Young Man*, 1974; and *The Court Years, 1939–1975*, 1980 (used by permission of the Douglas Estate).

SYNOPSIS OF SCENES

The action of this play occurs within the mind of a dying man.

(Except for the Intermission, the action is continuous, with each scene beginning as an abrupt time–jump.)

SETTING: There is no definite realistic scenery. The various times and activities of Justice Douglas' life are indicated by a few basic props and pieces of furniture: a wheelchair, a hiking staff, a Stetson hat, a judge's robe and chair, books and papers.

TO THE ACTOR AND DIRECTOR:

Douglas moves unquestioningly backward and forward through his lifetime. At each point, his memories quickly become the present reality.

The actor must convey the various ages of Douglas—from a child to a dying man of eighty-one—and must do so without any changes of makeup. In the opening and closing scenes, the lighting can help create an impression of fragile old age. Since the predominant scenes are those of his vigorous forties and fifties, the part could well be taken by an actor of that age. Those scenes of youth and childhood can be played for what they are: the self-persuasive memories of youth in the mind of an old man.

Though it would be a bonus if the actor were closely to resemble the late Justice, it is certainly not necessary. Far more important is conveying the physical essence of the man: his muscular, rather bear–like stance, his habit of combing through his hair with a paw–like hand, his tremendous, restless, nervous energy, revealed by such actions as drumming his fingers on the arm of a chair.

His speech is predominantly rapid and confident, as befits an urbane intellectual and man of action. Only occasionally is there a slowing: either in playing the role he has always enjoyed, that of simple rustic—or in a genuine faltering from deep emotion or bewilderment.

For Sue

For Sure

MOUNTAIN

ACT ONE

ACT I
SCENE 1
January 19, 1980

Darkness. The ferocious roar of a blizzard is heard.

MAN'S VOICE *(offstage):* Bill! Where are you?!

(The MAN'S *offstage voice moves throughout the theater—barely audible over the roar of the wind)*

DOUGLAS: I'm climbing!

MAN'S VOICE: You have to *wait!* Get *used* to these *heights!*

DOUGLAS: I'm climbing!

MAN'S VOICE: Let me *find* you! I'll help you *down!*

DOUGLAS: I don't need your *help!* I'll do this my*self!*

(A sudden shaft of light captures DOUGLAS, *who collapses against the wall. A moment of rage at his own incapacity—then he falls into unconsciousness.*

The MAN *now enters, outlined by a sinister shaft of light. He reads from a large ledger book. The unconscious* DOUGLAS—*ill, frail, aged—is caught in the nightmare we are witnessing)*

MAN: *Griswold versus Connecticut:* 1965. Supreme Court Justice William O. Douglas wrote the decision. There is a constitutional right to privacy. *(He rips the page from the book.*

A similar light suddenly strikes a WOMAN. *She also reads from a ledger book)*

WOMAN: *The New York Times versus the United States:* 1971. President Nixon may not stop *The New York Times* from printing the Pentagon Papers. *(She rips out the page)*

MAN: *Ballard versus United States:* 1946. No state jury system may discriminate on the basis of sex. *(Rips out page)*

WOMAN: *Furman versus Georgia:* 1972. The death penalty is cruel and unusual punishment. *(Rips out page.*

MAN *and* WOMAN *speak of* DOUGLAS *as if he weren't even there)*

WOMAN: He's obsolete.

MAN: My God, this is 1980!

WOMAN: He's irrelevant and his ideas are dying!

MAN: His ideas are *dead!*

WOMAN: He was never a true *Justice.*

MAN: Never a *scholar!*

WOMAN: Always going off somewhere to climb a mountain.

DOUGLAS: Climb . . . I was just there. The Himalayas. Just now!

MAN: That was a *dream.* Thirty *years* ago. Remember?

DOUGLAS: Remember? . . .

MAN *(matter–of–factly):* Jasper Crisbody.

DOUGLAS: Jasper . . .

MAN *(as* CRISBODY*):* Cleaning up the town. Making Yakima safe for my sons.

DOUGLAS: Bastard.

MAN: Close down South Front Street: the boot-leggers—the women.

DOUGLAS: Hypocrite.

MAN: Young man, your father was our minister. You help me now and I'll give you a dollar an hour.

DOUGLAS: No!

WOMAN: You spent your life saying no. A loner. Contrary. Always dissenting.

MAN: Always wanting to get away from the Court.

DOUGLAS: My life was the Court. Thirty–six years on the Court!

WOMAN: You wasted your time, wandering all over the world.

MAN: What were you trying to *prove?*

WOMAN: This is a nation of *laws.*

MAN: Not of *men.*

DOUGLAS: But the law must be about Life! About the people and *their lives!* How can you sit in judgment on them if you haven't *lived?* If you haven't taken those *journeys?* My life wasn't just one place—one case. Goddamn it! Multitudes! All things are connected.

MAN: And now you're dying.

DOUGLAS: Yes! I'm dying! *(A pause. With each beat,* DOUGLAS *becomes gradually more vigorous, in charge)* But that's not the *last* thing I'm gonna do. I've planned my own *funeral.* And it's going to shake up that damn Establishment. They're going to bury me at Arlington —got the spot all picked, not far from Jack Kennedy—and only twenty feet from Oliver Wendell Holmes. And there I'll be—among all those Generals and Secretaries of Defense. And you know what my tombstone is going to say? "William O. Douglas: Private, United States Army." *(Cackles)* And for the funeral, I'll have the U.S. Army Chorus sing, "Shall We Gather At The River." Right? And just when they're thinking that at the end, Bill Douglas got all soft, I'm gonna have that Army Chorus hit 'em with a song by Woody Guthrie, "This Land is Your Land"! By God, I just wish John Foster Dulles could be there. The blood would drain right out of that Episcopalian face. *(Laughs. Surprised at himself, calling offstage)* Tell those doctors I've decided not to die! *(To audience)* They're probably all Republicans! Oh, I gotta admit it: not *every* Republican is like John Foster Dulles. Some of the bastards actually have a sense of humor. Did'ja hear what Bob Dole called our last three Presidents—Carter, Ford and Nixon? Called 'em, "See No Evil. Hear No Evil. And . . . Evil!"

Well, and a lot of these Democrats today. They're no bargain, either. Bunch of weathervanes. Pisses me off. Some of those fellows think they're gonna be more conservative than a Republican. Can't be done. Like trying to be more ugly than a spider. You got to face the fact: Republicans and spiders have conservative and ugly *all locked up! (He laughs happily)* I'm feeling better! These goddamn doctors won't let me do *any*thing. Everything's "dangerous." Well, shit, of *course* it is. *Life* is dangerous. If you *live* it! *(Calls offstage)* And I've decided to *live!* Right up to the Bicentennials! The *real* ones. Not that thing that Gerald Ford had in '76—for the Revolution. Any fool country can have a revolution. But what *this* nation obtained was our Constitution and our Bill of Rights! They give life and protection to the minorities. And by that, I mean *all* of us. Every man and woman is a minority of one. And he and she, if it comes to that, must have the right to stand up to the full and awesome majesty of this Government, and say, *unafraid*, "Here is this small, humble area that is my life. And it *is mine.* So you, United States of America, get off my back!"

(In the passion of his memories, he has become a dozen years younger—vigorous and confident)

WOMAN *(as reporter):* You could have been President.

DOUGLAS: That's right.

MAN *(as reporter:)* You wanted it.

DOUGLAS *(thinks a moment, but makes no answer. Instead, he walks to where his black Justice's robe is hanging. He picks it up and holds it lovingly):* I wanted this. And they made me hang it up. But I made them sweat thirty–six years before I did it. Retire. Be safe. *(He shakes his head, and his mouth forms a mirthless smile)* Dangerous. *(He continues speaking)*

SCENE 2

1968—1975

DOUGLAS: Oh, they'd been trying to take this off of me as soon as I'd put it on. Especially after I'd made that awful mistake back in 1951. Said we ought to recognize China.

MAN: You mean "Red China."

DOUGLAS: Whatever you call them and whatever you think of their government, acting like one billion people aren't there is a fantasy. And fantasy is a mighty dangerous way to run your foreign policy. People like Richard Nixon said my suggestion was shocking. They stood up in Congress and said I ought to be impeached. The John Birch Society.

WOMAN *(as Birch member):* William O. Douglas is the only known Communist in Yakima County.

DOUGLAS: Twenty years later, I thought of that —watching those pictures of Nixon drinking champagne with Chairman Mao. *(In an Irish accent)* "History," Mister Dooley said, "history always vidicates the Dimmycrats. But niver in their lifetime. They see the truth first. But th' trouble is, nawthin' is iver of*fi*cially true, till a Raypublican sees it!"

MAN *(as Gerald Ford):* We're going to get Douglas off the Court!

DOUGLAS: Things got hot again in the Seventies. Nixon was trying to get G. Harrold Carswell on the Supreme Court. So he got a Congressman, Gerald Ford, to threaten the Senate.

MAN: If you don't confirm Carswell, we'll impeach Douglas.

DOUGLAS: On what grounds? Get this. Ford stands up in the House and says:

MAN: An impeachable offense is whatever a majority of the House of Representatives considers it to be at a given moment in history.

DOUGLAS: I know what was one of those "impeachable offenses." That I've been married four times.

WOMAN *(as citizen):* And your children never really had a father!

DOUGLAS *(angry and defensive):* They had more than *I* had. My father went and *died* on me. And I did all right. *Alone.* Didn't I?

WOMAN: Did you?

DOUGLAS: Christ almighty, you can't be everything. You have to choose.

MAN *(as critic):* Douglas is the kind of liberal who loves humanity in general, but hates people in particular.

DOUGLAS *(subdued):* You can't be everything! Least, I couldn't. *(Musing)* Four wives . . . Mildred. Merci. Joan. Cathy. My children . . .

MAN: A failure.

DOUGLAS: What do you know about somebody else's marriage?! *(Brooding, he mumbles something inaudible)*

MAN: *What?*

DOUGLAS *(after a beat, grudgingly):* Hell. Maybe you're right. . . .

WOMAN: A dirty old man.

DOUGLAS: Yeah? Well, *I* never had the chance to be a dirty *young* man!

WOMAN: A smut–peddler.

MAN *(as Ford):* Another of Douglas' impeachable offenses is that he is "involved with pornographic publications."

DOUGLAS: I don't know why it is, but Republicans are absolutely obsessed with pornography. Every chance they get, they buy a big stack of it and go off together to read and watch it and write a big report on why no one else should have a chance to do the same thing.

I remember one year at the American Bar Association, I shocked 'em by telling this story. It was about a judge who was asked to make a speech on Ancient Roman Law. Now he knew absolutely nothing about that subject, so he got his law clerks to write him a speech and he took a plane to the convention. But when he got there, he discovered he'd left the manuscript at home. Now there was no way he could improvise a speech on Ancient Roman Law. But the audience was all male, so he just winged it and gave a talk on sex. And his audience loved it. When he got back to his hotel that night, there was a message to call his wife.

WOMAN *(as wife):* Dear, you left your speech here at home. How did everything go?

DOUGLAS: Everything went perfectly, dear. I gave a talk on "How to Pilot a Small Airplane." Well, two weeks later, a fellow who'd been in the audience ran into the wife. He told her, "Your husband gave us about the best speech we've ever heard."

WOMAN: Really? That's amazing. Because you know, he's only done it twice. The first time, he threw up. And the second time, his hat blew off.

DOUGLAS: The fact is I myself cannot stand true hard–core pornography. But I know the First Amendment doesn't allow me to run around censoring it. Thank God. Because then I'd have to spend all my time reading the stuff— and, worst of all, *defining* it. Back in '71, I tried to explain that in one of my dissents. *(Reads)* "Whatever obscenity is, it is present only in the minds of some and not in the minds of others. There are as many different definitions of obscenity as there are men. And the definition is as unique to the individual as are his dreams."

MAN *(as other justice):* Douglas, this is an open–and–shut case.

DOUGLAS: I agree. The police illegally *open* the man's home and the Supreme Court unconstitutionally *shuts* him up in prison.

WOMAN *(as Voice of Court): Irvine versus California.*

MAN: The man's own words convict him. He was taking illegal horseracing bets. *(Gestures to file)* The evidence is all here.

DOUGLAS: And how did it all get "there"? Because the police—*without a search warrant*—
made a key to the man's home—bored a hole
in his roof—put microphones in his home.
What is this, a police state?

MAN: There is no constitutional right to privacy.

DOUGLAS: There *is*. You just don't *see* it.

MAN: Legal precedent, Douglas. And judicial re-
straint!

DOUGLAS: But the police must have a search
warrant!

MAN: Federal police, yes. Not state or local police.

DOUGLAS: But the Fourteenth Amendment: "No
State shall make or enforce any law which
shall abridge the privileges or immunities of
citizens of the United States."

MAN: That clause of the Constitution is a mere
inkblot.

DOUGLAS: An inkblot?!

MAN: No one knows what its authors intended it
to *mean*.

DOUGLAS: I know what it *says*. I can read the English language.

MAN: *Your* reading. You want to move away from *original intent*. Reinterpret the Bill of Rights!

DOUGLAS: That's our job!

MAN: You liberals! Thinking up new "rights" every morning for breakfast!

DOUGLAS: Because you reactionaries are *forgetting* some every night after your brandy!

MAN: You think your vision is superior to the Founding Fathers'?

DOUGLAS: What did the Founding Fathers know about electronic surveillance? About computer databanks? *Nothing!* History *moves*. And Justice has to move *with* it!

MAN: Can't you see how dangerous that is? You want to become a little god—unelected and appointed for life? You want to *choose* the freedoms we guarantee the people!

DOUGLAS: And *you* want to choose the freedoms we *deny* the people. *(To audience)* The Court is sending that man, Irvine, to prison. But I dissent. *Thou shalt not ration justice!*

MAN: But he's obviously guilty!

DOUGLAS: No! Guilt must be proven! The presumption of innocence is all that stands between us and the concentration camp! Hidden microphones. Illegal burglaries. This case will come back to haunt us.

(The MAN *and* WOMAN *turn from him and converse among themselves)*

WOMAN *(as citizen):* I'm absolutely appalled by the transcripts of those White House tapes. Electronic bugging. Burglaries.

MAN *(as citizen):* I'm seeing for the first time a Nixon I never knew existed.

DOUGLAS: Where the hell have you people been over the past quarter–century? *(To audience)* You're too young to remember this, but Nixon first ran for Congress in 1946. Someone pulled a "third–rate burglary" in his opponent's campaign office—stole all the campaign literature. Hired Hollywood actors to pass out that stolen literature.

MAN *(with a Russian accent):* We are Russians campaigning against Richard Nixon.

WOMAN *(outraged):* Well then, Mr. Nixon certainly has *my* vote!

DOUGLAS: Four years later, "someone" passed out photographs of his new opponent—a woman this time—doctored photographs that showed her hugging and kissing a black man.

WOMAN *(taking a "photograph" from* MAN*)*: My heavens! Mr. Nixon certainly has *my* vote.

(The WOMAN *and* MAN *shake hands)*

DOUGLAS: *I* first met Nixon in the Thirties. He was a student at Duke University and I gave a lecture there at the law school. Years later, he came up to me, in that patented way of his, and told me how important to him that lecture of mine had been.

MAN *(as Nixon):* Justice Douglas—I just want you to know that your lecture inspired my own political career.

DOUGLAS: I do believe that hearing that compliment was the most upsetting moment of my life. *(A beat)* God, I hate to admit it. But Nixon and I were a*like* in some ways. Western boys. Loners. Listening to the trains headed East. Climbing up to the top. However we could. *(A beat)* But now I've lived to be on the Court that's saying no to Richard Nixon. No, you *will obey the law.* Funny how things work out. The man who wanted to impeach *me* now has to leave Washington. And that's punishment for Nixon. I have to stay. And that's a punishment for me. Washington's no place to live. People in this town have no *roots.*

SCENE 3

1949—1957

DOUGLAS: *My* home's the *other* Washington—
three thousand miles away in the Pacific
Northwest. Every summer, I still ride up and
down the trails of the Cascade Mountains. Up
there, without any help from the politicians, I
very nearly *do* leave the Court. Autumn of
1949. Elon Gilbert and I are riding horseback
up Crystal Mountain, just across from Mount
Rainier. *(Looks up at sky)* Glorious day! Mountain's getting ready for winter: huckleberries
blood red and the willow and tamarack all
golden. My trail horse, Kendall, is a wonderful,
trustworthy old boy. We're heading up a grade
of sixty degrees. Something wrong with my
saddle. I dismount and tighten the cinch, but
after another hundred yards or so, Kendall,
(sound of a horse's frantic neighing) for what
reason I will never know, he rears up and slips
me off his back. I land in shale rock, lose my
footing and roll down thirty yards onto a nar-
row ledge, on my stomach. I raise my head and
I'm looking in the face of an avalanche.
Kendall! Sliding right down the same thirty
yards. Just got time to duck my head. Then
sixteen hundred pounds of solid horseflesh
rolls right over me. I'm hearing my own bones

break. First, I'm afraid I'm going to die. Then I'm afraid I'm not. Out of my twenty-four ribs, twenty-three are broken—in thirty-eight places. And my left lung is punctured. It takes over an hour for help to come, but it might as well be a century.

They lift me up into a litter. "Shoot me! Please God, shoot me!" And that's what they do— only it's morphine they shoot me with. I'm in and out of dreamland for five days.

Then mail—from all over the country. Get–well notes from people like Mercedes David-son. Beautiful woman. Wife of a diplomat. People like President Harry S Truman. And a letter from Harry E. Mock of Marion, Indiana.

MAN *(as Mock): I* broke three ribs once. And I just want to give you a pat on the back.

DOUGLAS: "Dear Mr. Mock: When you have twenty-three broken ribs, a hiccup is a crisis, a cough a disaster and a sneeze a calamity. But the most unfriendly act in the world would be a pat on the back."

MAN *(as doctor):* Douglas, you'll live. But your mountain climbing days are over.

DOUGLAS: Over? Doc, this summer, I'm going to cross the Himalayan mountains.

MAN: The Himalayan . . . that would be suicide!

DOUGLAS: But on mountain trails, I always take the *out*side edge. It has the best view.

MAN: And suppose you fall *off.*

DOUGLAS: Yes! Suppose I fall off . . . and *live!*

MAN *(after a beat, dismisses him):* Go ahead. It's your funeral.

DOUGLAS: Send wildflowers. *(To audience)* My trail partner's waiting for me in the Punjab. A Buddhist mountainman named Rahul.

MAN *(as Rahul):* My toes are frostbitten from last winter.

DOUGLAS: I have only one–and–a–half lungs. But we're going to walk 240 miles. Twenty days on trails above 13,000 feet . . . and up. Way up. The trek of the cripples. And off we go. On the trail we're joined by a caravan of eleven mules and five Shamanistic Hindus. The mules are draped with red and yellow tassels. And bells! *(Sound of bells)* As we walk above the clouds, what a din they make! Echoing from the cliffs —blown back by the winds. We go to tiny villages.

WOMAN *(as villager):* Here comes the caravan!

DOUGLAS: An old blind man sitting on a sunlit wall, beating his cane in time to the bells. *(Bells fade away)* Each time we leave a village, we climb up—up to one of the high mountain passes. And then the men in the caravan look up to the sky and shout.

MAN and WOMAN *(she as echo): Ki–ki so–so lha gyalo!*

DOUGLAS: "Let the gods conquer all the evil spirits!" You think that's primitive superstition? But I think it's like shouting, "Praise be to God!"

MAN *(as Rahul):* Today, we reach the pass at Staglang La.

DOUGLAS: The highest point on our trek— 17,489 feet. And there above us, mountains nearly 30,000 feet high. I remember the mountains of my youth—Mount Adams, so tall, so majestic. Yet here it'd be only a foothill. Let's all say it together!

ALL *(with echo): Ki–ki so–so lha gyalo!*

DOUGLAS: Hindus, a Buddhist and a Scots Presbyterian. *Ki–ki so–so lha gyalo! (Echo)* "Praise be to God!" No candles, no stained–glass windows. But the most beautiful church in the world. *Ki–ki so–so lha gyalo! (The echoes fade away)* That journey ends in Gilgit, a town just south of the Chinese border. Our last night, the border guards dress in long white pajamas and they dance for us. A dance I will never forget. *(A slow crescendo of drums begins softly)* Two men to start with, but others keep joining until there're about twenty. The sound of feet striking the earth is harder and faster than I thought possible. Primitive man, back at the beginning. I can't keep my feet still. I've seen the ice cliffs of Nanga Parbat. I've heard my prayer caught by the winds of the glacier. But above and beyond that, are the pounding feet of Gilgit, the dance that makes a man want to jump and whirl and stomp and join in a mad exercise of war and combat.

(Silence)

WOMAN *(as wife):* Time to unpack.

DOUGLAS *(a beat):* King David danced before the Lord. And he smote the Philistines. Me: I go back to Washington, D.C. *(Sounds of dinner party)* Back to a marriage of twenty-eight years that is dead. Long dead.

WOMAN *(as Mildred):* Bill, I'm not coming to any more of these things at the White House.

DOUGLAS: Jesus, Mildred. Roosevelt is *easy* to talk to!

WOMAN: I never know what to say to him.

DOUGLAS: Tonight that man spent one solid hour trying to talk to you. And you just *sat* there. Like some scared rabbit!

WOMAN: Can't you understand? I don't want to talk to a President.

DOUGLAS: Then who in God's name *do* you want to talk with?

WOMAN: With people I know and love. With our old friends back in New Haven. With our children. With *you.*

DOUGLAS: Maybe you married the wrong man.

WOMAN *(astonished):* No . . .

DOUGLAS: Do you have any idea how many women would *die* to be here in Washington at this time in history?

WOMAN *(after a beat, bitterly):* Yes, I'm afraid I do.

(She turns from him. A pause. DOUGLAS *turns to the audience)*

DOUGLAS: Mercedes Davidson. She makes me feel a*live.* Young! Gorgeous—*cultured* woman. The wife of a diplomat. Can talk to foreign leaders. To a President. The kind of woman who be*longs* here in Washington. Who was *bred* to move in the highest circles. *(A beat)* I *need* her.

WOMAN: I'm only standing in your way, Bill. I want to go back to New Haven.

DOUGLAS: Tommy Corcoran—who always wanted me to run for President—Tommy says the divorce business, that's the end of that dream.

MAN *(as Corcoran):* In politics you don't get a divorce. You have women, but you don't get a divorce.

DOUGLAS: How many rules can you break, before your ticket runs out? Shit. I'm sending Truman a letter, putting an end to any talk about the Presidency. I'm on the Court for life. And that's that. *(A beat)* Mildred got the divorce in '53.

WOMAN: Fifteen minutes before a judge and it's all over, never was—or one is supposed to believe it never was: twenty-eight years of devotion, loyalty and hard service. You are a famous and brilliant man. May God help you find it in your heart to forgive yourself, as our children and I do. With all good wishes. Mildred.

DOUGLAS: But our children *never* forgave me. They didn't under*stand.* Mildred, you never *grew.* You never seemed to *want* to. Not in the way *I* wanted you to. *(To audience)* Twenty–eight years. A di*vorce.* You can make explanations—excuses. My father would have called it a sin. *(A beat)* He would've been right. *(A beat)* But how could I stay in New Haven? Christ. How can I stay in Washington? I have to keep moving. Lebanon, Israel, Korea, the Philippines, Vietnam, Pakistan, Russia. We're a global power, but I don't think we have any real understanding of the rest of the world. I want to see it for myself—to talk with farmers and bus drivers and mountainmen. I take Mercedes, my new wife, and drive 7,000 miles in two months across the Middle East.

WOMAN *(as Merci):* From Karachi, Pakistan, to Istanbul, Turkey.

DOUGLAS: All in a two–tone green '56 Chevy station wagon.

WOMAN: On that trip, we lose five tires and six mufflers.

DOUGLAS: We have to replace the carburetor, the generator, a fan belt, the battery, three sets of points and a dozen spark plugs.

WOMAN: Then the gearshift rod comes loose, so we have to drive in second for 300 miles.

DOUGLAS: And we lose our side–view mirror when we're attacked by a homicidal Afghan sheep dog.

WOMAN: Otherwise, we have no trouble at all.

DOUGLAS: Merci and I divvy up the responsibilities according to our talents. I take the photographs.

WOMAN: And I repair the car.

DOUGLAS: Temperature: 110 degrees. Cross the Khyber Pass—through Afghanistan—then reach Tehran. We're honored guests in the palace of the Shah.

WOMAN: We meet the Minister of War—a man in his sixties, with a fierce black mustache and piercing eyes.

DOUGLAS: His name sticks in my mind: Amir Ahmadi.

(Soft sound of Persian stringed instrument. The three actors stroll amiably together)

MAN *(as Ahmadi):* Mr. Justice. Mrs. Douglas. What an honor you bring our poor country!

WOMAN: The honor is ours.

MAN: America has so much of everything. And we so little—except our problems.

DOUGLAS: But your country is a great bulwark of freedom. *You* are a champion of democracy.

WOMAN: That's why we have to help you solve your problems: poverty, disease.

MAN: And our troublemakers: the Communists. We need your help: resources, techniques.

WOMAN: But our visit here is unofficial.

DOUGLAS: We travel only as private citizens.

WOMAN: You've seen our car!

MAN *(laughing):* Even so, we must have your support.

DOUGLAS: You have it, General. *(Grips* MAN*'s hand)* Unwavering.

MAN *(to* WOMAN*):* Your husband is one of the few foreigners who understand us.

DOUGLAS *(to audience):* I feel my face burn with pleasure. Lawrence of Arabia. Douglas of Persia.

On a hilltop, only a hundred miles from the ruins of Babylon, I meet an old man. He tells me what happened in his village twenty years ago.

(Crescendo of wind begins)

MAN *(as old man):* That day, I saw a cloud of dust across the plain. It was an army troop galloping right at us, a colonel shouting orders. The soldiers dismounted and started shooting. They killed all the women and children. Everyone but the young men. I was shot in the neck. The body of my wife fell on top of me. I was covered in blood but saw what then happened. The colonel had the young men brought up, one at a time, to where a soldier stood with a sword. At each man in turn, the soldier would swing his sword. And just before it hit the prisoner's neck, the colonel would shout: "Run!" The headless man would take a step or two, then fall. They were betting on how far these headless men could run—laughing, shouting, encouraging those they'd bet on.

(Silence)

DOUGLAS: Did your people ever get revenge on that colonel?

MAN: That colonel became a general, and now is Minister of War. Amir Ahmadi.

DOUGLAS: I remember the garden of the Shah. *(Sound of Persian music)* I remember Amir Ahmadi—all his medals, his piercing eyes.

MAN *(as Ahmadi, to woman):* Please, Mrs. Douglas, do not think me a braggart. But the truth is, in my country, I am what you call a "household name."

WOMAN: Yes?

MAN: Oh yes. There are villages today where if a baby cries, the mother says, "Hush! Or Amir Ahmadi will get you."

(The music stops. The MAN and WOMAN freeze. DOUGLAS steps out of the frame and speaks to the audience)

DOUGLAS: And he laughed. Showing his golden teeth. Finally: back to Washington, D.C. *(Now with a sense of mission)* And I go to the *State* Department.

(MAN and WOMAN unfreeze. MAN is Under Secretary of State, shuffling and signing papers. WOMAN is executive secretary)

WOMAN: I'm so sorry, Justice Douglas. Secretary Dulles is all booked this week. But you *could* speak to Under Secretary Smith.

DOUGLAS *(turning to man who continues to shuffle papers sporadically, pretending to lis-*

ten to him): I've seen this pattern so often!
Foreign leaders flattering us—swearing their
love for democracy—feeding on our fears of
communism.

MAN *(professionally polite):* We're always grate-
ful to hear your opinions.

DOUGLAS: I know the opinions you hear. High–
level experts and businessmen, who never
leave our embassy except to go to the dicta-
tor's palace!

(MAN *walks to another part of the stage)*

WOMAN: I'm so sorry, Justice Douglas. But Under Secretary Smith has to go to a meeting
right now. But you might speak to Assistant
Secretary Jones.

(DOUGLAS *turns to* MAN)

MAN: Mister Justice, we have many channels of
information.

DOUGLAS: Channels of garbage! Fat cats telling
us exactly what we *want* to hear. And we *fall*
for it, over and over again. *Damn it, I* fell for it!

MAN: That shouldn't come as a surprise. You're
hardly an expert—

DOUGLAS *(interrupting):* But when a few of us
ask the *ordinary* people of the world: "What

do you want from America?" Oh, it's a different story! They don't want us policing the world. *We* ought to be the revolutionaries. Not the Soviets—that constipated, third-rate country we're so terrified of! We ought to aim at the *villages* of the world. Take one-*tenth* of what we spend on bombs. Bring their youngsters over here, show them how a town meeting works. We ought to send *our* youngsters over to those villages. With portable generators and water-purification equipment and medicine. (DOUGLAS *snatches a sheaf of papers out of the hand of the* MAN) This is our *chance*. Finally to *learn* from our experience. To use our *strengths*—not just our *force!* To become an *example*. Like a person who can *learn* from his failures. His *stupidities*. His *vanities*. And be *better* for it!

MAN (*taking back the papers from* DOUGLAS): Mister Justice, you really ought to take care of your own store. We are the experts on foreign policy. You're an expert on the *law*.

(*He walks away*)

WOMAN: *We* are the State Department. *You*'re an expert on the *law*. Remember?

(*She walks away*)

DOUGLAS: I remember.

SCENE 4

1934—1945

MAN *(as student, entering "classroom" embarrassed):* Sorry I'm late, Professor Douglas.

DOUGLAS: Sit down, Mr. Stuart. *(Looks around at "other students")* Gentlemen. *Muller versus Oregon:* 1908. Subject?

MAN *(looking about, then tentatively):* The right of Oregon to regulate laundries and factories?

DOUGLAS: Regulate what?

MAN: Whether women could be made to work more than ten hours a day.

DOUGLAS: Who argued the case for the women?

MAN: Louis Brandeis?

DOUGLAS: Very good. Why not someone else? *(Silence)* Because *no one else would take the case!* Why *not?* (Silence) Because the law—*as it existed*—was entirely on the side of the factories and against the women. So what legal citations did Brandeis make before the Court?

MAN: None, sir.

DOUGLAS: None?

MAN: Because there *weren't* any. Brandeis just argued the social and economic facts of life. And he *won.*

DOUGLAS: Exactly! He presented what we now call a "Brandeis brief." Reality! Life! Not just legal books. That's the kind of law we're *try*ing to *teach* you here at Yale. So where is Mr. Brandeis today?

MAN: On the Supreme Court, sir.

DOUGLAS: And thank God. *(A beat)* That's all today, gentlemen.

MAN *(getting up):* I'm sorry I was late, sir. Next time, I promise I'll be here *bright and early!*

DOUGLAS: Don't promise more than you can deliver. Just be here *early. (Walks to* WOMAN*)* Mildred, I love teaching these kids!

WOMAN: We can live here in New Haven the rest of our lives. In ten years, you'll be Dean!

DOUGLAS: Most of the country is suffering through the Depression.

Len Cariou as Justice William O. Douglas in the 1990 off-Broadway production at the Lucille Lortel Theatre, New York City.
Photo by Martha Swope

Len Cariou (left) with John C. Vennema in the 1990 off-Broadway production directed by John Henry Davis.

Photo by Martha Swope

Len Cariou (left) with Heather Summerhayes in the 1990 off-Broadway production. Set design by Philipp Jung, lighting design by Dennis Parichy.
Photo by Martha Swope

Len Cariou (right) with Heather Summerhayes (standing) and John C. Vennema in the 1990 off-Broadway production. Costume design by David C. Woolard.

Photo by Martha Swope

WOMAN: But our life is so happy, it's almost embarrassing.

DOUGLAS: Luck. Back in the boom years of the Twenties, I became a legal expert on bankruptcy. Now—when the whole country's bankrupt . . . I get this letter, from Washington, D.C. Chairman of the Securities and Exchange Commission. Man I've never met. One of the richest men in America. *(To* WOMAN*)* Joseph P. Kennedy.

WOMAN: Joe Kennedy?! What does *that man* want?

DOUGLAS *(a beat):* He wants me.

MAN *(as Joe Kennedy):* I want you to do a study on how corporations use the bankruptcy laws to cheat their stockholders and the public.

WOMAN: I'll stay here in New Haven with the children. It *is* just one semester? Isn't it, Bill?

DOUGLAS *(walking into Kennedy's office):* What do I do?

MAN: Goddamnit, don't *you* know? Maybe I've got the wrong man. I want you to find those bastards down on Wall Street and *get* 'em.

DOUGLAS *(to "staff"):* All right. There's only one way we can get this job done. We'll work from nine to six every day. Take dinner. Then come back here and work till midnight or after. Seven days a week!

WOMAN *(as staff member, exhausted):* We've finished the report, sir. All eight volumes.

DOUGLAS: And if I do say so—we get the bastards. And we're going to get more economic reforms through Congress than I'd ever dreamed. Because we catch the President of the New York Stock Exchange! *Richard Whitney!* Not with just his hand in the till, but his elbow, shoulder and half his butt! He's embezzled over a million dollars in bonds and cash from the Exchange's retirement fund. I take the evidence against Richard Whitney and bring it to the Oval Office. I hand it to FDR.

MAN *(as FDR):* No! Oh no, not Dicky Whitney!

DOUGLAS: "Dicky" Whitney and FDR were classmates at Groton and Harvard. Makes you wonder. If *I* were the crook, would Roosevelt weep over Billy Douglas of Yakima? *(A beat)* Well, give him credit. FDR dried his tears. And "Dicky" Whitney went to jail. *(Bemused)* I hear they're furious at me down on the Street. They don't understand. Christ, we're not trying to destroy capitalism. We're trying to *save* it from the *capitalists!*

(A telephone rings)

MAN *(as Brandeis):* Professor Douglas? Justice Brandeis speaking. I've been hearing about your work. Could you come to my home this Sunday? My wife will prepare us lunch. Do you like soup and boiled chicken?

DOUGLAS: I learn to *love* soup and boiled chicken. Louis Brandeis knows I exist!

MAN: What do you plan to do with the rest of your life, young man?

DOUGLAS: Go back to being Dean at Yale.

MAN: Oh no.

DOUGLAS: No?

MAN: No, you won't be permitted. You're a rising star in this town. Tell me. What do you think of FDR? Be honest!

DOUGLAS: He's magic.

MAN *(laughing):* He's a magician, all right.

DOUGLAS: A hero.

MAN *(sharply):* Listen, Douglas. Never depend on heroes. *Use* them. Keep your eye on the *window.*

DOUGLAS: Window?

MAN: Throughout history, great economic power and great political power are almost always like this. *(He interlaces his hands together)* Rarely, very rarely, you find an open window. And when you find that window, move like lightning! Once in a blue moon, someone *opens* that window *for* you.

DOUGLAS: Like Joe Kennedy.

MAN: A pirate. Who happens not to be in the old-school, Protestant inner circle.

DOUGLAS: Like FDR.

MAN: The greatest politician in America. And with polio.

DOUGLAS: Or you, Mr. Justice.

MAN *(ironically amused):* A Jew.

DOUGLAS: One of the greatest Supreme Court Justices of all time!

MAN: Oh my. I'm eighty-two years old, but I know one thing for certain. *You* are *not* going back to being Dean at Yale.

(BRANDEIS *walks away*)

DOUGLAS *(to audience):* Sunday, March 1939. Early spring in Washington. I'm at the Manor

Country Club, trying to learn how to hit a golfball. Maybe it'll help me get along better with Republicans. Then:

WOMAN *(as secretary):* Mr. Douglas. A call for you from the White House. President Roosevelt.

DOUGLAS: Driving there, I'm certain: He's going to ask me to run the Federal Communications Commission—which I want to do about as much as be mayor of Vladivostok. But how do you say no to FDR?

(He walks into "Oval Office")

MAN *(as FDR):* Bill, I have a new job for you. A mean, dirty, thankless job. (DOUGLAS *nods)* It's a job you won't like. (DOUGLAS *nods)* It's a job you'll detest. (DOUGLAS *nods)* Someone you know is retiring. He's asked me to let you replace him. Tomorrow, I'm nominating you to take the seat . . . of Louis Brandeis on the Supreme Court.

(DOUGLAS reacts: dumbfounded, ecstatic, proud. He touches the robe lovingly, then slowly puts it on)

DOUGLAS: I'm the proudest man alive. On the Court for *Life! (A beat)* For *Life!? (A beat)* I'm only *forty! (A beat)* But it's a hell of a window. And if *I* don't take it—?

(He turns to MAN. *They begin playing poker)*

MAN *(again as FDR):* Bill, do you know the two
things I like best about you? First, you're not
afraid of a damn thing! Two cards. (DOUGLAS
deals him two cards) You're just like my Elea-
nor. Both of you tell me exactly what you think
—even when I'm wrong!

DOUGLAS: I'm taking one card. *(He deals it to
himself)* Mr. President, not many people like
to be told they're wrong. Especially Presidents!

MAN: Then they don't belong here! *(Looking at
his hand, exasperated. Throws in his cards)*

DOUGLAS *(putting down his own cards):* Pair of
fives. *(A beat.* FDR *is rather annoyed)* Mr. President, you said you liked something *else* about
me.

MAN: That you play a goddamn maddening . . .
(A beat) but a rather interesting game of
poker! *(Deals cards. Nonchalantly)* Have you
ever thought of getting into politics?

DOUGLAS *(carefully):* Sir, I think the Court is
enough for any man.

MAN: Some men. For other men, there's no bid-
ding limit. Is there?

DOUGLAS: Depends, Mr. President, on which cards you're dealt.

MAN: Mmmm. *Some* men manage to win with a pair of fives.

DOUGLAS: Sir, I *play* cards. I don't try to read the future from them.

MAN: Very wise. After this war, though, we're going to need someone with vision. Someone who can connect with the common man. Who can *win*. *(A beat)* So how many cards do you want?

DOUGLAS: Mr. President: you're the dealer. *(He puts down his cards)* I'll take five.

(Distant music: "Happy Days Are Here Again." DOUGLAS *turns to audience)*

DOUGLAS: Roosevelt's running. Fourth term. Party bosses happy as hogs. But they've laid down the law: Dump Henry Wallace as Vice President.

MAN *(to* WOMAN*)*: Grace, take a memo. To Robert Hannegan, National Committee Chairman. "Bob: I will be thoroughly delighted to lead the Democratic ticket to victory in 1944. And at my side, as Vice President, I would be happy to have William O. Douglas—or your own man, Harry S Truman."

DOUGLAS *(obviously excited)*: My God! *(Musing)* "Roosevelt—Douglas." I've got to get a speech ready!

WOMAN *(as secretary)*: Mr. Hannegan? You wanted to see me?

MAN *(as Hannegan)*: Sweetheart, I want you to retype this letter. With these changes. Just reverse the order of those two names. OK?

DOUGLAS *(bitterly)*: Presto: FDR's first choice for Vice President:

MAN *(proud of himself)*: Truman.

(Music stops)

DOUGLAS: Roosevelt wins. *(Bitterly)* With Truman. *(A beat)* And we're winning the war. Every day, Roosevelt looks more exhausted. Frail. But no one wants to think about it. Late afternoon in April. I'm driving west on Constitution Avenue. *(Auto horn)* A friend's car. He's pointing at his radio. I turn mine on. And there it is: *(Muffled drums)* I park my car—somewhere near the Lincoln Memorial. And walk. I walk for hours.

(A pause)

WOMAN *(as reporter)*: You could have been President.

DOUGLAS *(suddenly furious with grief):* Damned son–of–a–bitch. Never *once* talked to me about his polio. Not *once!* Always the strongest, the healthiest man in any room. (A beat) Damn it: Why'd he go and *die* on me? Alone. Again.

(The drums have gradually faded away. DOUG-LAS has removed the robe and is sitting facing the audience)

SCENE 5

1898—1922

MAN *(as doctor)*: As a doctor, Mrs. Douglas, I must tell you the truth. Your son has contracted infantile paralysis. And he has lost the use of his legs. Permanently.

DOUGLAS: Permanently. That means forever. *(Ponders)* Permanently. But Mama starts giving my legs a rubbing in salt water. Fifteen minutes, every two hours. Oh Mama, that hurts!

WOMAN *(as Julia, trying not to cry)*: I know it hurts, Treasure. But don't cry. You're going to walk.

DOUGLAS: That's what she calls me: Treasure. For over a month, she sleeps in a chair next to my bed. Every two hours, day and night, she takes warm salt water and rubs my legs, up and down, for fifteen minutes.

WOMAN: When I was a little girl, I could run like the wind. *No* one could catch me. And that's the way you're going to be, too.

DOUGLAS: And then she laughs and rubs my legs: rub and rub. And two hours later, rub some more.

MAN (*as father, frail*): Son, when I get my strength back, I'm going to teach you how to ride a horse. They call this part of Washington "Horse Heaven," because of the grass. And if you ride up on a hill, you can see the Columbia River down to the south and, off in the west, Mount Adams.

DOUGLAS: It has snow on it, even in the summer. I gotta learn how to ride a horse. 'Cause I still don't walk very good. And maybe never will.

WOMAN: Just ignore those older boys.

DOUGLAS: Mama, let me wear long pants. Let me *hide!*

WOMAN: Oh, Treasure. That's just silliness.

DOUGLAS: Don't make me go back to school.

MAN: William! I never want to hear you say that again.

DOUGLAS: But those guys are always laughing at me. At my . . . legs.

MAN: Forgive them, Billy. They know not what they do. Didn't Christ tell us that?

DOUGLAS: Well, yeah. But maybe *you* should tell it to those *guys*.

MAN *(laughing):* I don't think any of them care to hear *my* sermons.

WOMAN: Billy, come indoors and rest now. You mustn't overdo and exert yourself.

DOUGLAS: Yes, Mama.

MAN: Billy, you *have* to get well. Because you're going to do all the things that I'll never do. Walk in places that I'll never see.

DOUGLAS: Yes, Papa.

MAN: Promise you'll never be afraid.

DOUGLAS: I promise.

WOMAN: Billy!

DOUGLAS: Yes, Mama.

WOMAN: Billy, your father's ill. We're going to have to carry him out to the wagon.

MAN: It's all right. The doctors know now. It's my ulcers.

WOMAN: They're taking him to a hospital in Portland, Oregon.

DOUGLAS: And he must go under the knife.

WOMAN: We don't need to worry now. The doctors say he's all better.

DOUGLAS: But . . . but then . . . *(He breaks into sobs)* Now who is going to teach me how to ride a horse?!?

CHORUS:
YES, WE'LL GATHER AT THE RIVER—
THE BEAUTIFUL, THE BEAUTIFUL RIVER—
GATHER WITH THE SAINTS AT THE RIVER,
THAT FLOWS BY THE THRONE OF GOD.

DOUGLAS *(over singing):* The funeral is in a big church in Yakima. We get in carriages and go up the hill to the cemetery. It's August and everything is dusty. Dry lumps of dirt hitting the casket. I'm holding Arthur by the hand. Mama and Martha are crying. But the minister bends down to me.

MAN *(as preacher):* Billy. You must be the man now.

DOUGLAS: I look at him and right there over his head, way off in the West, is Mount Adams. Up there, it isn't hot and dusty. Up there, it's all snow and clean. Nothing can make *it* cry or hurt or be miserable. Right then, I decide: there's nothing in the world I want more to be, than that mountain. That night, I dream that soldiers are throwing me, and all the other weaklings, off the top of Mount Adams. I wake up. Suddenly, an overwhelming light sweeps over me. I will make myself strong. Before they kill me, they'll have to catch me. *(He starts to walk again with great determination. A small breakthrough. He begins a gradual crescendo of ability)* I'll walk these foothills above us. First, without stopping. Then without a change of pace. Then, whistling as I go. Then, I'll run. I'm going to be strong! Every day—through school and then through college —I walk and run, till my legs and lungs are as strong as anyone's. Together now with my brother, we hike the Cascade Mountains.

MAN *(as Arthur Douglas):* Twenty.

DOUGLAS: Forty miles.

MAN: Through pine forest meadows.

DOUGLAS: Up rock walls.

MAN: Hey, do we have to climb it *this* way?

DOUGLAS: *Sure* we do. Come *on!*

MAN: I mean, there's an easier path on the other side.

DOUGLAS: Arthur Douglas! What in the blue hill blazes is *wrong* with you? Take the *easy* path?!

MAN: Maybe we wouldn't break our necks that way.

DOUGLAS: But that's the *point!* Why climb a mountain where you can't break your neck?

MAN: We'd get there just the same.

DOUGLAS: No, we would *not.* We'd get there like some . . . bunch of weaklings. Now I'm climbing this rock wall. Are you coming with me?

MAN *(looking up in resignation):* Lord, I guess.

DOUGLAS: Just keep looking *up!*

MAN *(terrified):* I'm not looking *down!*

DOUGLAS: All the way up to the glaciers!

MAN: Bill, you got blood on you!

DOUGLAS: Good!

MAN: Oh Lord, we're almost there!

DOUGLAS: Almost!

MAN: We're *there!*

DOUGLAS: The *top!*

MAN: We *did* it!

DOUGLAS *(near exhaustion. In pain, but exhilarated):* I did it. I *did* it!

WOMAN *(again as Julia):* Treasure: you have a beautiful *mind.* Let those *other* boys clamber up those mountains.

DOUGLAS: I'm a better climber than *any* of 'em.

WOMAN: You're a *teacher* now. Time to settle down.

DOUGLAS: High school English and Latin?!

WOMAN: Treasure, you can teach at Yakima High School the rest of your life. In ten years, you'll be the *principal.*

DOUGLAS: Yes, Mama. *(A despairing look at audience)* I owe her so much. I love Artie and Martha. And her. Oh God, I love these Cascade Mountains. *(A beat)* I've saved up seventy–five dollars. *(To* WOMAN*)* I've written New York City. Columbia Law School, Mama. They've accepted me!

WOMAN: New York City?! That's . . . too *far!*

DOUGLAS: No it isn't, Mama.

WOMAN *(stubborn, frightened):* It's too *far!*

(DOUGLAS *walks over and picks his mother up off the ground, her feet dangling in the air*)

WOMAN: Bill! Put me down!

DOUGLAS *(putting her back on the ground)*: Listen to me, Mama. Listen! *No* place is too far. *No* place!

(There is a pause)

WOMAN: Bill . . .

DOUGLAS: I'm leaving tonight.

WOMAN: Come pray with me.

DOUGLAS: I'm leaving tonight. For Wenatchee, Washington. *(Sound of train.* DOUGLAS *tenderly kisses the top of the* WOMAN*'s head. During the next speech,* WOMAN *exits)* Martha, my sister, will take care of Mama. I'm taking a Great Northern Railroad freight train to Chicago. My ticket's free, because I'm in charge of 2,000 sheep. Taking them to the Chicago stockyards. Nobody's ever heard anything more romantic than the clackety–click of those wheels in the cool night air. *(Sound of train abruptly stopping)* My God.

MAN *(as train crewman)*: It's a railroad strike, Sonny.

DOUGLAS: Twenty–four hours, we just sit, high and dry on a siding. These 2,000 sheep have to eat and drink! Every time the train stops, I have to get them on grass. North Dakota, we stop for two days.

MAN *(as crewman):* Shoot, we don't know *when* we're leaving.

DOUGLAS: I'm starving!

MAN: So hike down to the station lunch counter.

DOUGLAS *(to audience):* And that's what I do. Buy five dollars worth of food, pretty big bagful. And a whole apple pie. *(Train whistle. Then sounds of coaches moving, gradually louder)* My train! Heading east—with my 2,000 sheep!

(He runs, carrying "bag" and "pie")

MAN: Come on, you can make it!

DOUGLAS *(almost to the "caboose." He drops the "food"):* No! All that beautiful food!

MAN: Come on!

DOUGLAS *(jumping on board):* "Go east, young man!"

MAN *(as train conductor):* Chicago!

DOUGLAS: Well, mister, here's your 2,000 sheep.

MAN *(as stockyard official):* A little scrawny . . .

DOUGLAS: But I didn't lose a *one! (To audience)* Now I hitch a freight for the last leg to New York City. This time: no free passage. Some *other* guys are hitching rides. And we gotta pay each of the train crew fifty cents, sometimes a dollar.

MAN *(as crewman):* If ya don't, I'll turn you over to the yard–bulls.

DOUGLAS: Jesus! One guy didn't have any money. And those bastards threw him right off the train. *(Terrified)* Jesus. I think he broke his neck! I've got my jackknife, but . . . now the crews are changing just about every state. Each time, I have to fork over more money. We're going down the Hudson River Valley— the outskirts of New York.

MAN *(as conductor):* OK, kid. Ya owe me a dollar.

DOUGLAS: Have a heart, mister. I'm broke.

MAN: So jump off or I'll run you in.

DOUGLAS *(looking out of train, terrified):* Mister, just a few more miles!

MAN: Jump!

(Throws DOUGLAS *off train, who then rolls all the way down center. Whistle. Train sounds abruptly drop, then slowly die away)*

DOUGLAS: But I'm OK. Oh, I'm a lot more than OK. For the first time in my life I know, *really* know, what a monstrous huge country this is. And just how hard it can be. But God, I love it. And there at the end of the track are the buildings of New York City. I'm filthy, skinned and hungry. All I've got left is six cents. But I've put behind me now forever the weak, skinny–legged cripple I once thought I'd always be. So damn those bastards. I'm not afraid of them. I can do anything.

(Blackout)

END OF ACT ONE

ACT TWO

MOUNTAIN

ACT II

SCENE 1

1910—1922

Darkness. We hear an up–tempo rendition of a Western country song, played by a banjo, guitar and a folk–blues harmonica. Lights up. DOUGLAS *stands at center.*

DOUGLAS: My father—back in Washington State —conducted his first church service on a Thursday night in a one–room building.

His congregation was one man. Father waited ten minutes for anyone else to show up. Finally he said, "Well sir, there are only the two of us. Should we go ahead or should we maybe wait a week till the people know I'm here?"

The other fellow stood up and said, "Reverend Douglas, I'm not a preacher. I'm just a cowboy. All I know is: If I had forty horses and a load of hay—and I went out to feed them, but could find only one old horse—well, I don't think I'd let that horse go hungry."

Father was very moved, and he said, "Thank you. You've reminded me what my life is all about." And he went on to preach a sermon that lasted an hour. Then he shook hands with the man and asked him what he thought.

The man said, "Reverend Douglas, I'm not a preacher. I'm just a cowboy. But if I had forty horses to feed—and when I went out looking for them with a load of hay, I found only one old horse—I don't think I'd give him the whole wagonload."

Maybe I'm giving *you* too much of a wagonload. But I can't help that. It all comes together. I'm a preacher. Like my father. Like Louis Brandeis. See, they both preached sermons about the *real problems* of *life.*

I guess my father was the only preacher in town who did. The only one who cared about the itinerant workers. Some were Wobblies: Industrial Workers of the World.

MAN *(as preacher):* We mustn't let our children be contaminated by this human scum.

DOUGLAS: That's what the other ministers in town said. But Father was right. Those people weren't scum. I *know* because after he died, I had to work right alongside those people. One day—I was around fifteen—I picked four hundred pounds of black cherries.

MAN *(as orchard owner):* OK, kid. Here's your pay.

DOUGLAS *(resigned):* Four dollars. If I'd bruised the fruit, I wouldn't have gotten a dime. No minimum wage in those days.

MAN: And damn sure no unions.

DOUGLAS: Saw the sheriff meet a union organizer at the railroad station and drag him out of town behind a motorcycle.

MAN: We run things in this town because we know what's good for you.

WOMAN *(as Julia):* Treasure, that's why God put them on the top.

DOUGLAS: That's what Mama thought, bless her. Well, we weren't on the bottom—that level belonged to the Yakima Indians. But we Douglases sure weren't on the top. Wrong side of the tracks. Too poor to have birthday parties. Too poor to be invited to anyone else's.

MAN *(as citizen):* Jasper Crisbody.

DOUGLAS: Jasper . . .

MAN: Cleaning up the town.

DOUGLAS: No!

MAN: I'll give you a dollar an hour.

DOUGLAS: NO! *(A beat. Reflecting on these un-imaginable riches)* A dollar an hour . . .

WOMAN *(again as Julia, with dignity and pride):* We never had any money. But we were never *poor*. We're Douglases. We ex*cel*.

DOUGLAS: Or *else*. In my high school, I was vale-dictorian. "Man loves God best by serving Man." Earned a full–tuition scholarship of one hundred dollars a semester to Whitman College in Walla Walla.

I'll never forget one professor: Dr. Benjamin H. Brown. He taught physics and geology. And a cosmic view of life. Over in Europe, the World War had started.

MAN *(as Dr. Brown):* Millions of young men are being killed. But whatever men will do, the earth will still grow wildflowers. The Alps and the Cascades will still stand. Look at this: a human skull. I discovered it one day while digging around an apple tree. The roots had grown through the eyes, sucking the entire brain into the tree. Think of it. Whoever this skull once was, has now become an apple tree!

DOUGLAS: None of us could think of an afterlife more choice.

(Martial drums and music)

DOUGLAS: The summer of 1918, doing close–order drill: left, right, left, right. Private Douglas.

MAN *(as citizen):* Fighting for democracy.

DOUGLAS: Then the news.

WOMAN *(as citizen):* The Armistice!

DOUGLAS: Damn!

MAN *(as sergeant):* All right, you men! None of you've gotten any closer to France than goddamn Spokane! But get inta your goddamn uniforms. Because you're gonna parade right down the middle of goddamn Walla Walla!

DOUGLAS: The crowd's euphoric. It's like a beautiful dream. Men throwing their hats in the air. Women rushing into the street to embrace us. We're heroes! *(Music very faint)* After the parade, I strut around town in my uniform. Then, as I start into a drugstore, I bump into Logan Wheeler's girlfriend. I'd known Logan for years. He'd worked at his father's creamery, then got shipped to France and was killed in the Argonne Forest. I can't remember her name. *(Remembers)* Ruby!

(WOMAN *turns.* DOUGLAS *proudly salutes. She begins to weep and walks away*)

MAN: Big Hero in his uniform.

(Music has stopped)

DOUGLAS *(bitter, ashamed):* Hero. *(A beat)* Yeah. There's a guy named William Borah. A senator from Idaho. Who heard a Negro was going to be lynched by a mob outside of Boise. He hired a locomotive to take him there and shamed that mob into letting the law take its course. *That*'s who I want to be like. *(Sound of train, quietly rattling down the tracks. Sound continues throughout scene)* Then one day, a train passes through town. Filled with men the government's arrested. Wobblies. Thirty or forty men in each car. No food or water or toilets. Just sealed boxcars. *(A beat)* A man who takes no interest in public life isn't harmless. He's *useless.*

MAN *(as Wobbly, with a harmonica):* An idea that ain't dangerous ain't worthy a bein' called an idea at all. *(Plays a chord or two on harmonica)*

DOUGLAS *(startled):* What?

MAN: Where you *head*in', kid?

DOUGLAS: Chicago. I'm taking all these sheep to the stockyards. Where *you* headin'?

MAN: *De*troit. I'm an organizer.

DOUGLAS: Union?

MAN: IWW.

DOUGLAS: Yeah?

MAN: Ever met a Wobbly before?

DOUGLAS: Sure.

MAN: That right? What makes a kid like you leave the Cascade Mountains? For a junkyard like Chicago?

DOUGLAS: Not stayin' in Chicago. Goin' on to New York City.

MAN *(laughing):* Ain't real sure that's much of a step *up*wards!

DOUGLAS *(proud):* I'm goin' to Columbia University! To the Law School!

MAN: The *Law* School! Well, if *that* don't take the blue ribbon!

DOUGLAS: Think I'm lyin'?

MAN: Naw, kid, I don't think you're lyin'. I'm just a little tickled. How life always throws you a fast one. See: Here we are. All cozy and friendly–like—ridin' a freight together. But someday—maybe we'll meet again. Me still an organizer. You a lawyer–boy.

DOUGLAS: Yeah?

MAN: And you know what'll happen.

DOUGLAS: What?

MAN: You'll do your job. Lock me deep away in Joliet Prison.

DOUGLAS: Aw, that isn't—

MAN: Now come on, kid, admit it. Don't that take the blue ribbon?!

(He plays a chord or two on harmonica. A pause. Train sounds finally die away)

DOUGLAS *(to himself)*: "A idea that ain't dangerous . . . ain't worthy a bein' called an idea at all." *(To audience)* And the same thing is true of a life. Teaching at Yakima—I was safe. *(He smiles)* And I wanted to be dangerous.

SCENE 2

1940—1953

DOUGLAS: If I'd known then what I know now! No group worships safety more than lawyers. And the safest place of all is right here: the Supreme Court!

MAN *(as Voice of Court): Minersville School District versus Gobitis.*

DOUGLAS: 1940. Fascism is on the march everywhere. And winning. That's when we get this case about two Pennsylvania schoolchildren. Ten and twelve years old.

WOMAN *(as Lilian):* We're Jehovah's Witnesses. We're forbidden to salute the American flag. "Thou shalt not bow down thyself to any graven image."

DOUGLAS: The Court has to choose. Religious freedom. Or the right of the state to demand respect for the flag. Eight of the nine members of the Court—including all of us Roosevelt appointees—we decide in favor of the state. Our flag is the symbol of our national unity—our national security. The only dissent is a Coolidge Republican—the man who was my Dean at law school: old Harlan Stone.

MAN *(as Stone):* The Government cannot force these children to express a sentiment which violates their deepest religious convictions. The Constitution is a command that freedom of mind and spirit must be preserved. It is a command which *Government* must obey.

DOUGLAS: Hugo Black and I, we aren't looking at each other. Can we have been that wrong? Where are the immutable principles of law that I thought were chiseled in granite? I ask the oldest member of the Court. Charles Evans Hughes, nearly eighty. *(To* MAN*)* Sir, since I joined the Court last year, you've been like a father to me.

MAN *(as Hughes):* Douglas, the safe and easy cases get settled in the *lower* courts. Up here, at *this* constitutional level, we get only the *dangerous* ones. Where ninety percent of any decision is emotional. The rational part of us merely supplies the reasons for supporting our gut feelings.

DOUGLAS: I feel the earth move under me.

(Loud telephone ring)

WOMAN *(as Martha):* Bill? It's Martha.

DOUGLAS: Martha! I've just been thinking—I'm so busy, but I just have to write you and Mama—

WOMAN *(interrupting):* Bill! You have to come home.

DOUGLAS *(a beat):* Of course I'll come.

WOMAN: Julia Fisk Douglas. 1872 to 1941.

DOUGLAS: President Roosevelt sent a wreath of red roses. Mother would have found that hard to believe. She'd been a lifelong Republican. But she came to Washington to see me sworn into the Court. And at a luncheon that day, she suddenly turned to me.

WOMAN *(as Julia, old):* You know, this man Roosevelt has got something to him after all.

DOUGLAS: They buried her next to Father. In that cemetery I'd avoided for forty years. It's green now, with tall trees blotting out Mt. Adams. The night I caught that sheep–train headed East, she said goodbye.

WOMAN *(as younger Julia):* You're as smart as your father. And maybe as good. But you'll never be as handsome.

DOUGLAS: She had high standards. *(Looking at grave)* Mama. *(He tries to speak, but it's impos-*

sible. Then:) FDR has just lost *his* mother. *(A moment's pause)* We both know something about strong mothers. *(Pause)* More and more talk about me running with him on the ticket in '44.

MAN *(as reporter):* So you want to leave the Court.

DOUGLAS: No! But a President . . . has the power to do the things that need doing!

WOMAN: And your marriage?

DOUGLAS: That's what the magazines want. *House and Garden* and *Ladies' Home Journal.*

MAN *(as Billy):* Dad! Can I talk to you?

DOUGLAS: Not now, Bumble. There's a magazine reporter here to photograph us. *(To magazine photographer)* You got color film in that camera? Mildred, you stand next to the kids. *(Puts on hat)* Bet you never saw a Supreme Court Justice wearing a Stetson! *(Whisper)* Mildred. Millie's slip is showing! *(Football)* Bumble? Go out for a long one. *(Throws a pass. Delayed, amused disappointment)* Awwwww! Good thing that boy's probably going to be a *lawyer!* Huh, Mildred? Come on. Give us a kiss! Children?

WOMAN *(as magazine reader):* The perfect American family.

DOUGLAS *(the happy mask drops like a curtain):* A lie! And it takes time away.

WOMAN *(as reporter):* Think he's running?

MAN *(as reporter):* You watch. He'll be on the ticket.

DOUGLAS: No! I don't have time for anything but the *Court!*

MAN *(as General):* A Jap's a Jap. They're a dangerous element, loyal or not.

WOMAN *(as citizen):* That's testimony by the general of our Western Defense Command.

DOUGLAS: The case has come to us.

MAN *(totally American accent):* My name is Gordon Hirabayashi. I was born in Seattle on April 23, 1918. I'm a Quaker, a member of the YMCA and a senior at the University of Washington.

DOUGLAS: The Army has sentenced you for refusing to report to your relocation camp.

MAN: Concentration camp—with barbed wire. That's where my parents are now. They used to have a roadside vegetable and fruit stand, south of Seattle.

WOMAN *(as citizen):* You can't trust them. They're *born* that way.

MAN: This order for the mass detention of all persons of Japanese descent denies America's democratic standards. Therefore, I must refuse this order for evacuation.

DOUGLAS: You represent a military threat to America. The Army and the Justice Department *say* so.

MAN: The ACLU has refused to take my case.

DOUGLAS *(to himself):* Everyone has turned his back on him.
(Reading column in paper) Westbrook Pegler.

WOMAN *(reading Pegler):* "The California Japanese should be under armed guard to the last man and woman. And the hell with habeas corpus!"

DOUGLAS *(reading column in paper):* Even Walter Lippmann.

WOMAN *(reading Lippmann):* "The West Coast is a battlefield. And the Constitution doesn't give our enemies the right to live and do business on a battlefield."

DOUGLAS: I know what the public wants.

WOMAN *(as reporter):* If you want to be Vice President!

DOUGLAS: Can't let that affect me. And I *don't want* to be Vice *Pre*sident!

WOMAN *(insinuatingly):* You know what to do . . .

DOUGLAS *(defensively):* What I'm saying is, you have to believe our military. This is *war*—declared by Congress.

MAN *(as Hirabayashi):* Then why aren't you filling those camps with *German*–Americans? *Italian*–Americans?

DOUGLAS: It's war! The Rape of Manchuria—Pearl Harbor—the Bataan Death March. We—the Court decides—

MAN: And you join the decision.

DOUGLAS: I—the Court. . . . *We* send the young man to prison.
(A pause)
Roosevelt's won his fourth term. *(Bitter)* With Harry S Truman.

MAN and WOMAN *(as reporters):* Not you.

(A pause)

DOUGLAS *(grimly):* No.

MAN *(as Billy):* Dear Mr. Justice Douglas.

DOUGLAS: Bumble? Why are you writing me a letter, Bumble?

MAN: I'm writing you a letter because you never listen to me when I talk to you.

DOUGLAS: That's silliness. Of *course* I listen—

MAN: You never listen when I talk—or *try* to talk to you about something important. This letter is about something important. It's not about the world or the nation or even about the law. It's only about me. Mr. Justice, I have decided not to go to law school.

DOUGLAS: Billy!

MAN: I have decided not to go to law school because I hate the law. To me, the law is everything that's evil in the world. The law has taken you away from me, from Millie and from Mother. And if you'll forgive me—it's taken my father away from himself. It's taken him into a world of compromise and politics. So please accept the fact: I'm not going to law school. Instead, I have decided to be utterly and ridiculously irresponsible. I am going to

try to become an actor. And if, Mr. Justice, that embarrasses you, I'm not sorry. Because that only proves you have forgotten the father that once took all of us on a long, wonderful train trip out West. One whole week we spent, just us together. No phone calls or reporters. No law. We played gin rummy together and you told us stories and played us cowboy songs on your harmonica. And I was happy and truly—
Your son,
William O. Douglas, Jr.

(A pause)

DOUGLAS: A letter: to William O. Douglas, Jr. I haven't got *time.* And you're wrong about the law. *(A beat. A shift in mood)* And wrong about me. You'll see. *(A pause)* A letter: American Bar Association. We're the most powerful nation in history. Yet we live in fear. Terrified of a few thousand members of the American Communist Party—a rag-tag group who couldn't elect a county dogcatcher from the Atlantic to the Pacific coast.

WOMAN *(as citizen):* You're defending *Communists?!*

MAN *(as Voice of Court): Dennis versus the United States.*

DOUGLAS: Yes. Before us, are eleven leaders of the American Communist Party. Why?

WOMAN *(as citizen):* Because they're *Communists!*

DOUGLAS: But Truman's Justice Department hasn't charged them with sabotage or terror or sedition. Not even of conspiracy to overthrow our government. Only with *teaching* the *writings* of Marx, Lenin and Stalin. Can the Court say, "Send 'em to jail"? Can we set aside the First Amendment?

MAN *(as Frankfurter):* Because of a "clear and present danger." We mustn't jeopardize the *Court.* We mustn't get embroiled in the passions of the day.

DOUGLAS: You know what that makes us? Like those bankers who'll give you a loan only when you don't *need* one. Sure, we'll give you justice. If you don't *need* it very much.

MAN: People get *justice* from *God.* From the *Court,* they get the *law.*

DOUGLAS: But this time we can give them *both!* We only *got* this case because every lawyer and judge in America is scared shitless of being branded a Commie! Hugo Black and I—I guess our necks are on the block. Because we dis*sent.* But the Court does the "safe" thing: sends those men to jail. *(A beat)* We need courage now. Because the problem isn't accusing innocent people of being Communists. The problem is stripping constitutional rights away from *any* American—including *Communists*. *(A beat)* There's a questionnaire being given to government employees.

WOMAN *(as investigator):* Do you have any records of music by Prokofiev?

MAN *(as investigator):* Any prints by Picasso?

WOMAN: Do you think blood plasma of Negroes should be mixed with that of whites?

MAN: Should the French get out of Vietnam?

WOMAN: Would you vote for Justice William O. Douglas if he ran for President on the Communist Party ticket?

DOUGLAS: We're a fast–moving people. But has anyone ever moved faster than I have in one year—from "Father Of The Year" in the *Ladies' Home Journal (A beat)* to Communist conspirator?

MAN *(as citizen):* Communist *spy!*

DOUGLAS: All right, I'll give you ten minutes. I've heard all the *other* lawyers. But it won't do any good. You know what I think? I think Julius and Ethel Rosenberg are guilty as hell. I think they were Communists *and* spies and conspired to pass along secrets of the atomic bomb to the Soviets.

MAN *(as lawyer):* We agree.

DOUGLAS: You *agree?* Then what—?

MAN: They shouldn't be executed.

DOUGLAS: Well, tomorrow they go to the electric chair. Unless you've got new evidence. . . .

WOMAN *(as lawyer):* A point of constitutional law.

DOUGLAS: I see . . . fascinating . . .
(To audience, excited) Fascinating! The Rosenbergs were convicted and sentenced to death by a judge. Yet the law says—for the crimes they committed—that only a *jury* can assign a death penalty. That didn't happen here.

WOMAN: Why didn't the Rosenbergs' own lawyers make that argument in appeal?

DOUGLAS: I think Stalin *wants* the Rosenbergs to die in the electric chair. I think he wants martyrs to the Noble Cause. The hell with that. Today, I've issued a stay of execution. Let the *whole* Court consider the point this coming October.

I'm heading West for the summer.

MAN *(as announcer):* Supreme Court Chief Justice Vinson has overturned William Douglas' stay of execution for atomic traitors Julius and Ethel Rosenberg.

DOUGLAS: Vinson, you can't *do* that! It's never been done! Oh, I know: The traitors have to die *now* and the hell with legal niceties. It's a fever in the land. But we don't have to catch it ourselves. We have to *cure* it. Well—I dissent from this decision.

"Our country must be protected against spies who would destroy us. But before we allow human lives to be snuffed out, we must be sure —emphatically sure—that we act within the law. No man or woman should go to death under an unlawful sentence merely because his lawyer failed to raise the point."

Hugo Black and Felix Frankfurter join in my dissent. Eisenhower is silent. That evening, Julius and Ethel Rosenberg are electrocuted.

And I'm dropped from the social register. A resolution is introduced in Congress to impeach me: I've given aid and comfort to the Communists. A traitor. When I meet old friends in the street—*(To* MAN*)* Lyndon? (MAN *turns his head and walks by him.* DOUGLAS *shrugs. He puts on his Stetson hat. To audience)* Time to get out of Washington.

SCENE 3

1953—1954

DOUGLAS: I spend the next ten days with a fellow named Harry Truman. *Not* the President Harry S. Just plain old Harry—a thoroughly disreputable mountain goat who runs a lodge up in the foothills of Mount St. Helens. Not more than forty miles west of Mount Adams. Together, we climb up St. Helens. And God, it is beautiful! Wildflowers everywhere. The one I love most—all alone, above the timberline, right against the snowdrifts: the avalanche lily. Clear white with a core of deep orange. That one, you can't transplant. It's allergic to gardens and all such comfortable places. It wants a raw wind and icy water. It thrives on them.

Harry! How does it feel to live your life on a volcano?

MAN (*as Harry*): Bill, you know the answer to that better'n *I* do. Hell, compared to that Washington, D.C. place, this old mountain's plenty solid enough for me.

DOUGLAS: At least, it is *today*.

MAN: Well, if it wants to, after I'm gone, this whole damn thousand acres can blow itself to the moon for all I care.

DOUGLAS *(to audience):* But I don't know about that. If you love all this, like I do, how can you not care what'll happen to it tomorrow? I always think of something said a hundred years ago by Chief Seattle of the Cascade tribes. He wrote a letter to President Franklin Pierce.

WOMAN *(as Chief Seattle):* If all the beasts were gone, men would die from great loneliness of spirit. For whatever happens to the beast happens to man. All things are connected. Whatever befalls the earth befalls the sons and daughters of the earth.

MAN: Bill, the problem is them Wall Street fellows!

DOUGLAS: *Uh* uh. A Soviet chemical factory'll poison a lake just as fast as one of ours will. And a Brazilian bulldozer flattens a forest just as eternally. No. The problem is Man. The kind of man who looks at a river and sees a dam. Who looks at a tree and sees lumber. Who looks at a mountain and sees gravel.

MAN: Then we're shit outa luck!

DOUGLAS: No! We make a mess. We can clean it up. What we need is another Bill of Rights— one that gives standing in court for our natural resources.

WOMAN *(as critic):* There you go again, Douglas! Riding one of your hobbyhorses and turning the law upside down.

DOUGLAS: Upside down?! You think that hasn't already happened? For the Almighty Dollar? Look at the Fourteenth Amendment. Created to protect the black man and woman—to make them first–class citizens. And what did the Court do after Reconstruction? Turned the law ass–up–in–the–air! Suddenly decided that corporations—*corporations!*—were people! Used the Fourteenth Amendment to stop any attempt to regulate the factories and the railroads. By God, if a corporation can be a person, then why in hell can't our trees and rivers have their day in court? A Wilderness Bill of Rights. *That's* what we need. And our grandchildren need it. And the planet needs it. Christ, imagine! What if we end up with nothing on earth, but . . . *people!?*

MAN *(as critic):* I was wrong. That man hates humanity in *general,* too!

DOUGLAS: I go back to the Capital. And what do I find? All the powers–that–be, including the Washington *Post,* cheerful as hell about destroying the Chesapeake & Ohio Canal. It doesn't make a profit, so the Establishment's decided to pave it over and make another highway!

To the Editors, Washington *Post:* The C & O Canal stretches 185 miles from D.C. all the way to Cumberland, Maryland. John Quincy Adams broke the ground for it. Maybe it isn't wilderness. But it's *green.* And generations of locals have walked alongside its muddy waters. I therefore challenge all of you to a hike: 185 miles—from Cumberland to this smog-choked city. *(Picks up hiking staff)* By Jesus, they accept. And off we go! Every community we pass through sends a delegation out to meet us. Here come trucks—full of radio and TV crews. You know, that's pitiful?! These days, it's become news when somebody actually *walks* somewhere. We make it back to town. And the *Post* changes its editorial mind. Now some people are calling for the canal to be turned into a national park.

WOMAN *(as wife):* Time to unpack.

DOUGLAS: I've built a home in the foothills of Mount Rainier. I'm planting clover on the hillside and something powerfully strange happens to me. Off in the distance, I hear the baying of hounds. Something brushes my leg. *(Turns)* It's a deer—a doe—exhausted, panting, her eyes dilated. Incredible. But desperate, with nowhere else to turn for help, she's come to a *human.* The hounds are sounding closer. *(Snaps fingers)* "You come with me." I walk a half–mile, with her at my heels like a puppy. Then we reach the river and I give her a pat on the rump. She dives in and swims to the other side. In a minute, the hounds arrive at the edge of the river. Furious. Their quarry has escaped—has been delivered over into freedom.

Whatever happens to the beast happens to man. All things are connected.

SCENE 4

1954—1975

SINGER *(very soft and distant):*
STEAL AWAY, STEAL AWAY,
STEAL AWAY TO FREEDOM.

DOUGLAS *(over song):* Beast and man. A century ago, one in every eight Americans was legally considered a beast, a slave, to be bought, sold and disposed of at the whim of its master. To end that scourge, a dreadful war was fought.

WOMAN *(as southern citizen):* Segregation is constitutional. We're separate, but we're equal.

DOUGLAS: *Plessy–Ferguson:* 1896. That slimy piece of hypocrisy. That dirty bargain to cancel the outcome of the Civil War.

MAN *(as Voice of Court): Brown versus Board of Education.*

DOUGLAS: A perfect case. With Earl Warren as Chief Justice, we finally have a majority. Five of us are now opposed to segregation.

MAN *(as Frankfurter):* But this is a momentous decision. We have to be unanimous.

DOUGLAS: That's where Warren makes the difference. Former Republican governor, an attorney general, a tough criminal prosecutor. One by one, the others join us. Warren announces a unanimous decision. May 17, 1954. The day we finally begin to keep some promises.

MAN *(as Warren):* Segregation is wrong, it's stupid, unconstitutional and it's time to stop it.

WOMAN *(as citizen):* Impeach Earl Warren!

DOUGLAS: Communities, whole states dig in their heels. Resist the law of the land. One man alone could prevent that. The most popular man in America—President Dwight David Eisenhower.

MAN *(as citizen):* But Ike sent in the troops to Little Rock!

DOUGLAS: That was to stop a riot—not to stop segregation. Ike never says one word to support the Court's decision. He walks away from us. Ten years of potential progress: down the drain. And all that is the paralysis of fear. Fear of what the black man and woman might do with their full share of American freedom. Booker T. Washington said it a long time ago:

MAN *(as Booker T. Washington):* "You can't keep a man down, unless *you* stay down *with* him."

DOUGLAS: Wherever you find a persistent sense of futility—particularly among the young men —with nothing really to gain from doing right and nothing really to lose from doing *wrong*— *that* is where you're going to find violence. When are we as a nation going to wake up to that fact? When?!

MAN *(as official)*: When are *you* going to wake up to the real dangers we face?

DOUGLAS: The State Department is trying to deport a man. A homosexual.

MAN *(as psychiatrist)*: Like all those . . . persons, he's a psychopathic personality.

DOUGLAS: That's what they call him—the State Department. And the Court—over my dissent —lets the bastards deport that man who'd come to us for justice. Psychopathic personality! Communist! Bolshevik! Names! Labels! Fear!

The first homosexual I ever knew, I met sixty years ago. In college, back in Washington State. I liked that fellow: good sense of humor, good friend. I suppose if I'd been asked to name the ten men I most admired, he would have been on the list. But one day, he touched my hand and said, "I love you." Could have said—I *should* have said—"That's *fine*" and changed the subject. But what did I know? I was an ignorant fool in a different world. What I did was push him away and walk out. Never spoke to him again. Avoided him. Fear. Fear!

And now we've got a President who's built his entire career on peddling fear.

WOMAN *(as Voice of Court):* Congress shall have power to declare War.

DOUGLAS: *That's* the Constitution. But for years now, Richard Nixon has been secretly bombing Cambodia. We're not at war with that country. Yet he hasn't informed the American public, the Congress, or even many of the responsible leaders of the Pentagon. Sending those men false military reports!

MAN *(as Nixon):* National security! Executive privilege!

DOUGLAS: But the Cambodians know you're bombing them. The Chinese, the Soviets all know. You're only lying to the American people!

MAN *(as Nixon):* They're like children. They don't *want* to know the truth. And we have to keep the Commies guessing. Let 'em worry, you know? That maybe I *am* insane—capable of anything. Let the mothers tell their babies: "Hush! Or Richard Nixon will get you!"

DOUGLAS: And he laughed. *(A moment's pause)* I am reinstating a lower–court order stopping this unconstitutional bombing. "The law of the land applies equally to this Court, to the resident of the ghetto and to the big white house on the hill." *(Pause)* Every single other member of the Court votes to reverse my order.

WOMAN *(as citizen)*: Douglas is paranoid!

MAN *(as citizen)*: Senile!

WOMAN *(as citizen)*: Degenerate!

DOUGLAS: I get a tape recording in the mail. Martin Luther King in the bedroom.

MAN: *Now* what do you think of your . . . "preacher"?

DOUGLAS: I'm convinced: the White House is electronically bugging our conference room in the Supreme Court.

WOMAN: No American President would do such a thing.

DOUGLAS: No?

MAN *(as Voice of Court)*: *Laird versus Tatum.*

DOUGLAS: We hear the case. Our Presidents have used the *U.S. Army* to snoop on Americans—on people working for civil rights and against the war. I find against the Government. "This is a cancer in our body politic. If we allow an intelligence officer to snoop over the shoulder of every nonconformist, this is no longer the America of Jefferson, but the Russia of Stalin." But the Court backs Nixon five–to–four. The fifth vote is his latest appointee. Young man named William Rehnquist. My God! Hugo Black is gone. Now Earl Warren is dying in Georgetown Hospital. I've got one hope. That Nixon will overreach. *(Roar of blizzard wind. Blinding light)* I remember a day in the Himalayas: 16,000 feet altitude.

MAN: Move slowly, Bill. You gotta get used to these *heights!*

DOUGLAS: Those rules were made for *other* men. Not me! I feel like Superman. *(The wind and light abruptly stop)* I took one more step and passed out for an hour.

MAN *(as Voice of Court):* Oyez. Oyez. Oyez.

DOUGLAS: It's happened.

MAN: *The United States vs. Richard Nixon.*

DOUGLAS *(with difficulty breathing):* July 6, 1974. The Supreme Court rules unanimously —William Rehnquist abstaining—that Richard Nixon must obey the law. That he must give the tapes to the Special Prosecutor. In less than a month, he's resigned. *(Calling out. He is jubilant, but clearly—and for the rest of this scene—an exhausted seventy-six–year–old man)* This is a special Christmas! Everybody. *Every*body on my staff gets an extra–long holiday. We deserve it! *(Softer as if to one person)* Cathy—I've got the tickets. Tonight, you and I are going down to Nassau!

WOMAN *(as Cathy, with mild humor):* No we're not, Bill.

DOUGLAS: We're not?!

WOMAN: My school. Important test on Monday. Something called . . . constitutional law?

DOUGLAS: But—

WOMAN: I'm sorry, but you'll have to change the tickets to Tuesday.

DOUGLAS: All right. *(To audience, admiringly)* What a girl!

WOMAN: Hey!

DOUGLAS: Right, right. Woman. *(A beat)* Cathy, why *do* you put up with an old *goat* like me?

WOMAN: Bill, at every party we go to, at least one attentive young man asks me that same question.

DOUGLAS *(slightly angry)*: They do?!

WOMAN: And I'll tell you what I say to them. That the men I most like are either under the age of five or over the age of sixty. Those are about the only times that a man really *listens* to a woman.

DOUGLAS *(pleased, but hides it. A beat)*: Sorry. What did you say?

WOMAN *(laughing)*: Bastard!

(They laugh and hold each other)

DOUGLAS *(looking out as from a balcony)*: Don't think I've ever seen water so beautiful. *(Visibly droops with exhaustion)* Darling, you know what things are like New Year's Eve. Please go downstairs and see about our dinner reservations.

WOMAN: Of course. You stay here. *(A beat)* Time to unpack.

DOUGLAS *(sighing happily but is drained. Looks about)*: Where did I put my razor kit? Ah, here it—*(Sudden light.* DOUGLAS *falls in a distorted pose, an amazed, uncomprehending look on his face. He calls out in little more*

than a whisper) Cathy. Cathy. (WOMAN *and*
MAN *enter with wheelchair. They lift him on
to it. He is very weak)* A stroke. All right—
stroke. But I'll be—back on Court. Gone
through—*(a pause)*—worse this. But no psy-
cho—neuro—logic—exam. No. No! *(He wheels
himself upstage, taking the judge's robe)* I can
read. Can write. I'm staying—the Court.
Counsel—my question—to you—*(A long,
painful silence)* My question—to you—*(*DOUG-
LAS' *face works with the confusion and frus-
tration of his inability)*

MAN *(as Counsel, puzzled, looks about him):* Sir?

DOUGLAS *(incapable. Finally):* Thank you. For
your spih—your spirited—argument.
*(Another pause. Then looks up as if at some-
one by his chair)* All of you. All my—friends.
Betray me. Tell me quit—be coward. Resign!
To Gerald Ford!! Be *nothing!* The Court—
that's my *life.* A *public life.* Even if—only half
—man. I can—cast a vote! The fifth vote out of
nine! And that vote can open the windows—or
close them! For all your *life*time! Someone—
has to stand up! For the—fruitpickers!

*(He begins to laugh grotesquely at himself, but
the laughter quickly turns to sobs of rage. Gradually, the tears subside. His face clears into a
huge blank sadness. The* MAN *has taken the robe
from him and thrown it on the floor.* DOUGLAS *is
the man we saw at the beginning of Act I)*

SCENE 5

January 19, 1980

(Until the last moments of this final scene, DOUGLAS *will slowly progress from a crippled, aphasic stroke victim to a vigorous and articulate advocate. Nevertheless, he is eighty-one years old and that should be consistently conveyed)*

MAN *(as bureaucrat, almost whispering, smug):* We got Douglas off the Court! Thirty–six years! But we got him.

DOUGLAS: Seek . . . *(Groping for thought. Furious. To "law clerk," snapping fingers)* Poem. The poem!

WOMAN *(as clerk, baffled):* What poem, sir?

DOUGLAS: Ancient . . . Persia . . . *(Pain)* Oh, Christ! *(Mental struggle)* Harmony! Disharmony.

WOMAN: "All anxiety comes from the search for harmony. Seek *dis*harmony. Then you will gain peace."

DOUGLAS: Yes! He under*stood!*

MAN *(as bureaucrat):* We got Douglas off the Court.

DOUGLAS *(despairing):* They want harmony.

WOMAN: *Every*one wants harmony, sir.

DOUGLAS: Mistake! *(Forcing words out)* Hitler. Stalin! Harmony!

MAN *(as Citizen):* We all want law and order.

DOUGLAS: But not . . . through harmony. Not everybody . . . everywhere the *same.* No!

WOMAN: *Dis*harmony, sir?

DOUGLAS *(with bitter humor):* Like my life.

MAN *(as reporter):* Four wives. Two of them young enough to be *grand*daughters! Why don't you write a book? *Douglas Tells All!*

DOUGLAS: All my . . . private life?

MAN: Human interest!

DOUGLAS: Gossip!

MAN: The dirt!

DOUGLAS: Like . . . *(Snaps fingers)* Case? Case?

WOMAN: Sir?

DOUGLAS: The case . . . *(Remembers) Irvine.*

WOMAN: *Irvine versus California.*

DOUGLAS: Yes. *(Beginning to hit his stride)* February, 1954.

WOMAN: The police wanted evidence against Mr. Irvine. They made a key to his home. Bored a hole in his roof—

DOUGLAS: Put a microphone in the bedroom where he slept . . . with his wife. Arrested him. Ransacked his home. Without a search warrant.

MAN *(as critic):* The Supreme Court found that his rights had *not* been violated.

DOUGLAS: Over my dissent! Constitutional liberty must include privacy. The right to be left alone . . . is the beginning of all freedom. *(Snaps fingers)* Case?

WOMAN: *Griswold.*

DOUGLAS: *Griswold. State of Connecticut:* 1965. Still a crime for a married couple . . . to use birth–control devices. A majority of the Court now agrees with me. I write the opinion.

WOMAN: "We deal with a right to privacy—"

DOUGLAS *(joining in, takes over. This decision, he knows by heart. He closes his eyes and recites):* "—older than the Bill of Rights—older than our political parties, older than our school system. Marriage is a coming together for better or worse, hopefully enduring, and intimate to the degree of being sacred."

WOMAN *(as Merci):* Bill? Why are you leaving me, Bill?

DOUGLAS: Merci?

WOMAN: You're destroying all we had together. Why are you leaving me for that child?

(DOUGLAS *is silent*)

WOMAN: We could be together the rest of our lives. You're on the Court—for the rest of your life!

DOUGLAS: No! I have to keep climbing!

WOMAN: Bill, I don't like what's happening. But I'm a *grown*–up, I can *live* with it. Why a *divorce?*

DOUGLAS: Because I *love* her!

WOMAN: You love her. Oh, poor Bill. You're really an old–fashioned boy, aren't you?

DOUGLAS: You don't understand!

WOMAN: You don't have to *marry* this girl.

DOUGLAS: She's not "this girl." Her name is Joan. She's a fine, educated woman. She's helping me with my research. My books.

WOMAN: And she thinks you're the greatest man alive. (DOUGLAS *is silent*) I *love* you, Bill. If you have to be *worshipped*, don't you have your law clerks for that?

MAN *(as critic):* Maybe you're a great Justice. But you're a pretty ridiculous old man.

DOUGLAS: Shut up!

MAN: A foolish old man. Chasing after young flesh.

DOUGLAS: No! *(A beat)* With Joanie . . . maybe. Yes! But not with Cathy.

MAN: Chasing after a dream of youth.

WOMAN *(as Cathy, a waitress):* Hi! What would you like?

DOUGLAS *(turning to her. Baffled, then slowly relaxes):* I think I'd like a smile. (WOMAN *smiles)* No. *(Smiles)* Nice smile. But not what I meant. A "smile" is a glass of your best Scotch in the house.

WOMAN: All right.

DOUGLAS: Bring yourself one, too. Sit down. Talk with me—Cathy, is it?

WOMAN *(sitting with him):* I'm putting myself through college. Waiting on tables. Not exactly a Fulbright. But 'twill serve.

DOUGLAS: Not one of those rich little bitches in a private school.

WOMAN: My father's a railroad worker.

DOUGLAS: Here in Oregon?

WOMAN: But I want to travel. See new places. New people.

DOUGLAS: Don't I know it?! How old are you?

WOMAN: Twenty–three.

DOUGLAS: Same age I caught a train headed East. *(To audience)* Sweet girl. Smart as a whip. Oh, she can run like the wind . . . *(Confused, in pain)* Damn. Sometimes . . .

WOMAN *(as Julia):* I know it hurts, Treasure.

DOUGLAS: Cathy?

WOMAN: Who is Cathy?

DOUGLAS *(bewildered):* I don't know, Mama.

WOMAN: No other woman in your life will ever call you "Treasure."

DOUGLAS: I know.

WOMAN: You must keep yourself clean and pure.

MAN: Just like Jasper Crisbody.

DOUGLAS: I don't want to think about him.

MAN: You've never *stopped* thinking about me.

DOUGLAS: Bastard! High and mighty church deacon!

MAN: Protecting my sons. Cleaning up Yakima.

DOUGLAS: Hypocrite!

MAN: I just want to close down South Front Street. The bootleggers. And . . . the women.

WOMAN: Say, aren't you the cute kid!

MAN: Saturday and Sunday nights. I'll give you a dollar an hour.

DOUGLAS: I was fifteen. More money than I'd ever seen in my life.

MAN: See if you can get one of those women to solicit you.

WOMAN: Aren't you the cute kid!

MAN: Sell you some white mule. Then you swear an affidavit and the police will move in.

WOMAN *(to* DOUGLAS*):* I know why you did it, you little bastard.

MAN: I'm going to make this town clean for my sons.

WOMAN *(to* DOUGLAS*):* Saving yourself for Jesus!

MAN: Good work, Bill. *(Exits)*

DOUGLAS: NO! No more! I quit!

WOMAN *(to* DOUGLAS*):* But you kept the money, didn't you? *(Exits)*

DOUGLAS *(he starts to reply to her, then shouts after the departed* MAN*):* Hypocrite! You're all alike! Hypocrites! *(He is alone. A long pause)* That young man. Gordon Hirabayashi. I sent him to *prison. (A beat)* Bill? So glad you didn't become a lawyer. I respect you more than any man I ever knew. I must *tell* you that someday. *(A thought)* I've got a jackknife for you. Somewhere. And I'll play you cowboy songs on my harmonica. Take the *time. (Increasingly bitter)* Before all the young men die. Before all the wildflowers die . . . *(He stops in agonized thought, then bitterly, sardonically quotes himself, the Bill Douglas of fifty-eight years before. He is now very old)* "I can do anything." *(A beat)* All those years. All that work. For nothing. Nothing! Everything falling backwards. Downhill. Maybe I should just have been an old man *(With bells and echo: Ki–ki so–so lha gyalo!)* sitting in the sun, beating a cane against the wall in time to the bells. Waiting to become . . . an apple tree!

(A pause)

MAN *(as doctor, from offstage):* Douglas, your mountain climbing days are over.

DOUGLAS *(a bellow of defiance):* Nooooooooo! Thou shalt not ration justice! Thirty–six years on the Court. I held the Constitution in my hands. And who's going to hold it tomorrow? Some goddamn eunuch?! Bought and paid for by the goddamn corporations?! You gonna let him destroy the Constitution? Invade your mind? Invade your bedroom? Dictate how many children you have? Just because he looks like a "nice family man" on television? Ask yourself! Do you think it really matters what Alexander Hamilton did in bed? Whether

James Madison was happily married? It mattered to *them*. To their *intimates*. But to *us*? To us, they gave a constitutional nation. Isn't that enough? Goddamn it, do you have any idea what leadership means? Climbing a mountain, every day, every hour. And if you're truly out front—alone—then *you* are the mountain you're climbing. Discovering yourself as you find the path, inch by inch. And no "hero" can do it *for* you! Because the fight is never won. But lost and won—over and over again. By YOU! *(Distant sound of wind)* Listen! Hike up the Allagash River in Maine. Smell the sweet grass: *Hierocloe.* "Sacred grass." You walk in acres of it and the whole world smells of vanilla. Yet take a handful of it to your nose and the smell is gone. Nothing. You need endless fields of it—next to free–running water. *(Ecstatic. He has found the core idea of his life. Sound of wind and the white light begin to intensify)* That's why we need wilderness! Wilderness in the world around us. Wilderness in the world inside us. Inside every man and woman, there's a wilderness, unique and sacred. Pave it over. Chop it down. And we all die!

The light is dazzling one moment—then blackout.

THE END